TIMELESS BIOGRAPHIES

THE GUTSY GIRLS WHO LED INDIA

WRITTEN AND ILLUSTRATED BY
ILINA SINGH

DESIGNED BY
ISHA NAGAR

HarperCollins*Children's Books*

First published in India in 2024 by HarperCollins *Children's Books*
An imprint of HarperCollins *Publishers* India
Building no 10, Tower A, 4th floor, DLF Cyber City,
Phase II, Gurugram, Haryana - 122002
www.harpercollins.co.in

2 4 6 8 10 9 7 5 3 1

Text © Ilina Singh 2024
Illustrations © Ilina Singh 2024

P-ISBN: 978-93-5489-967-6
E-ISBN: 978-93-5489-934-8

Ilina Singh asserts the moral right
to be identified as the author of this work.

The views and opinions expressed in this book are the author's own and the facts, verified to the extent possible, are as reported by her. While every effort has been made to ensure the accuracy of the facts presented, the publishers are not liable for any inadvertent errors that might have crept in. The illustrated maps inside the book are an artistic representation of present-day India and are meant only to give readers more insight into the lives of the women leaders.

All rights reserved. No part of this publication may be reproduced, stored in a retrieval system, or transmitted, in any form or by any means, electronic, mechanical, photocopying, recording or otherwise, without the prior permission of the publishers.

Portrait illustrations: Ilina Singh
Design, layout and other illustrations: Isha Nagar

Typeset in Josefin Sans 11pt/15

Printed and bound at Nutech Print Services - India

HarperCollinsIn

To gutsy girls everywhere, and to Nani

Preface

Anyone can be a leader. And everyone can learn to become a better leader. Walk into any bookstore and you'll find enough books on leadership to fill a shelf. Indeed, we are lucky to be born at a time when we have access to learnings from a variety of leaders across the ages and regions.

We are especially fortunate to be living in India, as our country has had many brave and inspiring leaders. I'm sure you've met some of these – from ancient kings like Ashoka and Chandragupta Maurya to freedom fighters like Bhagat Singh and Gandhiji – in your textbooks.

However, have you heard of Rani Abakka or Queen Didda? Probably not. Unfortunately, the ladies are often missing from these textbooks. Well, it's time to tell their story. In this book, you will meet ten Indian women who led their communities with courage, skill and wisdom; fought against the societal expectation of females to be meek and mild; and to this day inspire us to believe in our abilities and rise to face challenges.

Say hello to the Gutsy Girls Who Led India.

Of course, we will not be mounting our horses and charging into battle anytime soon, although that would be fun too. Instead, I hope this book encourages us to borrow a little inspiration as we think about our goals and how we can achieve them while also helping those around us.

For this, I have also developed a simple nine-step leadership framework after studying the leadership lessons we can take away from these inspiring women leaders. Good leaders live these lessons in their lives every day, and so can we all.

The lessons are gender agnostic – boys will, hopefully, find them equally useful.

There are two ways of enjoying this book – poetry and prose. Poetry brings alive stories almost magically. Prose is simple, easy to read and helps delve into historical detail. So, there's a poem on each leader, followed by their story in prose. You may choose to read these in the order that you prefer and then move on to the leadership lesson and activity.

Here's to the leader in you! I can't wait to see the wonderful things you are about to do.

Contents

Nine Steps to Leadership — 8

Queen Didda — 10

Gaidinliu Pamei — 18

Velu Nachiyar — 26

Abakka Chowta — 34

Ahilyabai Holkar — 42

Keladi Chennamma — 50

Mai Bhago — 58

Rani Lakshmibai — 66

Begum Hazrat Mahal — 74

Rani Durgavati — 82

Nine Steps to Leadership

Whilst everyone's journey of discovery will look very different, I found that there are nine important steps along the way to becoming an effective leader. Each step asks us to pause and reflect on a certain value, skill or intention. I'm sure you have come across some of these in life already! In isolation, none of them are particularly rare or challenging. However, when you are able to practise them together over time, you will see how your ability to lead and work with others is strengthened by these skills.

At the end of each chapter, I have provided a short activity that will make you think a little deeper about what you want to accomplish and how you can approach your goals. Try to complete the tasks as honestly and openly as possible to unlock your true potential!

Queen Didda

There was a king in Cashmere
Who prayed for a child, an heir;
To take over the royal crown
And rule over every hill and town.

A bonny baby girl soon arrived
But the unhappy king just sighed;
His heart full of anger and shame
For the child was sadly born lame.

The King's love shrivelled and dried
The child was insulted and deprived;
Destiny broke this sorry spell
When Princess Didda married well.

Her husband made her an equal partner
Royal coins had pictures of both him and her;
Queen Didda was clever and cunning
She quickly learned the tricks of ruling.

When her husband took ill and died
Didda was heartbroken and cried;
Her refusal to join him in the pyre
Earned her the wicked ministers' ire.

She became regent to her young son
And got rid of her enemies one by one;
Alas, her son too did not live long
Yet Didda's regency continued strong.

She groomed her three grandsons
Unfortunately, they died quite young;
She took the throne and became Queen
The fiercest one the land had ever seen.

Ruthless and ruling against all odds
She quelled revolts and exposed frauds;
Love her or hate her, but the fact remains
Peace and prosperity adorned her reign.

Art, religion and culture were inspirations -
In one year she laid 64 temple foundations;
When she finally died at the ripe age of 79
Her kingdom was strong, and her legacy fine.

Step 1: Self-awareness

Wouldn't you agree that imperfect characters, who achieve greatness despite their flaws, make for the most interesting stories? Queen Didda of Kashmir has a life story filled with action and adventure and many twists and turns. Luckily for us, an author and poet named Kalhana wrote a book titled *Rajatarangini* on the lives of the kings of Kashmir, in which he recorded her remarkable tale.

In the year 924 CE, a baby girl was born in the house of the King of Lohara, Simharaja. (Lohara lay in the Pir Panjal mountain range, on the route between western Punjab and Kashmir.) The girl was also the maternal granddaughter of the very powerful King of Gandhara, near present-day Kabul. Despite her noble birth,

Coins with Didda's name and portrait have been discovered in Kashmir.

Queen Didda was one of the longest reigning Indian monarchs. Her rule lasted over forty years.

Didda's life was not a bed of roses.

Legend has it that Didda, though very beautiful, was lame. Although this was not her fault, it made her father dislike her. Her early childhood was sad, and her future seemed uncertain. Her father married her off to the King of Kashmir, Ksemagupta, to bind the two kingdoms together in an alliance. This marriage proved to be a blessing in disguise for Didda.

Didda was a quick learner and adapted well to her new position as Queen. She won her husband's trust and respect, and he soon began to consult her in official matters. When he issued royal currency, he made sure coins were minted with Didda's name and image as well. The court was filled with several courtiers and ministers who tried to influence royal affairs to serve their own selfish interests. Didda's growing influence did not sit well with these ministers — they resented a woman becoming so powerful.

Didda's husband, the King, was very fond of a luxurious life. He especially enjoyed fox hunting. Upon his return from one such hunting expedition, he fell ill and died. Didda was suddenly alone amidst powerful, ambitious ministers who expected her to commit sati. But she refused to jump into her husband's pyre when the time came, and stated that her only child, young Abhimanyu, needed his mother. With the help of a kind minister, she placed

Abhimanyu on the throne. Since the boy was young, Didda effectively ruled as Queen Regent.

Didda had to swiftly get rid of the cunning and rebellious elements that threatened her. She used rewards, punishment, negotiations and sly divide-and-rule policies to break up the ministers and courtiers who tried to destabilize her. So effective was she in doing this, that she was accused of witchcraft since it was unthinkable for society to credit a woman with superior political skills.

Didda's ruthless side took a backseat after her son passed away from ill health. She plunged into sorrow and decided to honour his memory by building a temple in his name. She laid the foundation of several temples at this time and took it upon herself to repair old temples and monasteries.

Didda's three grandsons ascended to the throne one by one, but none of them lived long. After the death of her last grandson, Didda took the reins of the kingdom in her own hands. This made her one of the few female monarchs in Indian history. Her rule was long and ushered in a period of peace and stability in Kashmir. She died at the ripe old age of seventy-nine in the year 1003 CE. Before dying, she selected her brother's son as her successor to the throne. Even today, the legend of Queen Didda lives on as young people rediscover her rollercoaster tale.

Didda was born with a deformity in one leg that caused her to limp. This was considered an ill omen at the time.

Activity

Be Self Aware

Queen Didda used her sharp mental skills to overcome the physical challenge presented by her deformed leg. She did not let her limitations define her. Instead, she identified and developed her mind as a strength.

Before we set out to change the world, we need to understand ourselves well. We will be better leaders when we are tuned into what makes us tick. Knowing our strengths will help us power our journeys and understand the unique magic we add to the world. Also, knowing our weaknesses will help us work on them and find partners who can complement us.

Let us start your leadership journey by knowing more about you:

To download the activity PDF, scan this QR code:

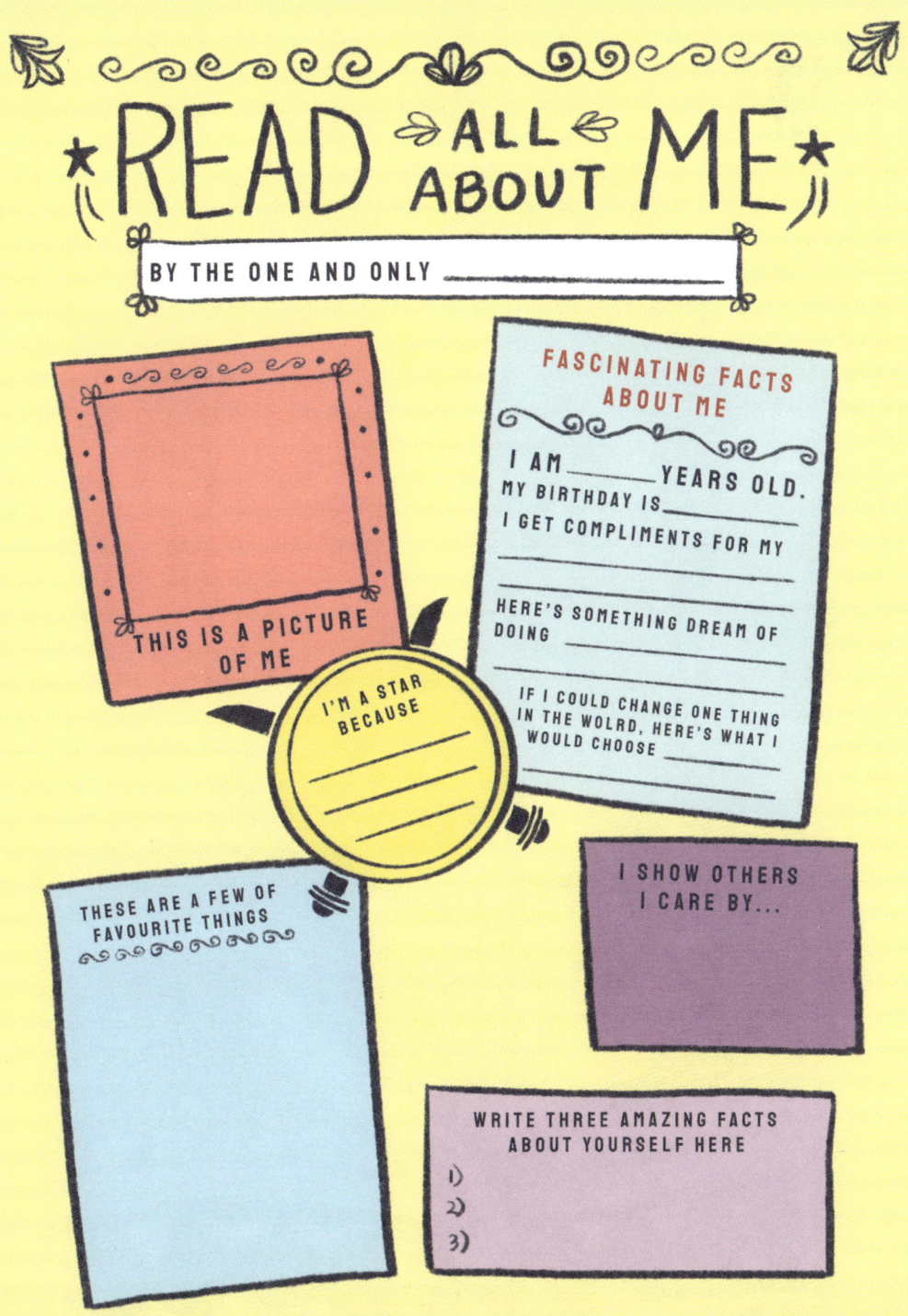

Gaidinliu Pamei

Now let's take our marching band
To the northeastern state of Nagaland;
It's not a state visited by many
But it's as important a place as any.

In this state seen by the lucky few
Was born the great Queen Gaidinliu;
With a spiritual strength rarely seen
She joined the Heraka at only thirteen.

Heraka was a movement of the Naga -
It was both a religious and political saga;
So dazzled were the Nagas by her prowess
That Gaidinliu was soon declared goddess.

Heraka soon took up the difficult stand
Of driving out the British from Nagaland;
The girl helped her cousin, who led at first
Till the British caught him and did the worst.

The child could have wallowed in sadness
But instead, got up and held the harness -

Of the Heraka and of the noble mission
Of sending back foreigners, of the vision,
that united her people into a coalition
the four tribes running the administration.

Resisting the attack on her dearest traditions
She fought the forced religious conversions
The terrible, harsh labour and the high taxations.

For three years she bravely led the resistance
It made the British worried and rather tense.

She was only 16 when caught and sent to jail
And was freed in 1947, when the Brits set sail;
She continued serving her people, she never sat still
Nehru praised her as "Rani" and "daughter of the hills".

Step 2: Purpose

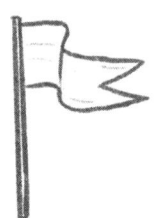

Rani Gaidinliu was born on 26 January 1915 in Tamenglong district in present-day Manipur.

As you already know, India won her independence from British rule as a result of many sacrifices by several men and women across the country. One remarkable story that's seldom told is that of Rani Gaidinliu. She was born on 26 January 1915 in the Tamenglong district of present-day Manipur in the Rongmei tribe (also known by the name Kabui).

When Gaidinliu was little, she saw the British exploiting the people and resources of her land and forcing the people to convert to Christianity. Gaidinliu belonged to one of the three Naga tribes that made up the ethnic group called Zeliangrong. This group of people worshipped the Supreme God Haipou Tingkao Ragwang or Tingwang. Little Gaidinliu loved her culture and wanted to protect the religious and social uniqueness of her land.

When Gaidinliu turned thirteen, she joined her cousin Haipou Jadonang's Heraka movement. While initially this was more of a spiritual movement aimed at resisting foreign interference in local religious and cultural practices, over time it expanded into political protests, and aimed to unite the Naga people against the British.

When her cousin was captured and executed in 1931, Gaidinliu took charge of the Heraka movement at the age of sixteen. She led the guerilla forces that fought against the British. She led an armed revolt in Nagaland, Manipur and Assam. She encouraged her people to stop paying taxes to the foreigners and take pride in their tribal identity and religion. This made her one of the few women leaders of the Indian Independence Movement who actively fought the British. She became a target of the government, and search operations were launched, where soldiers hunted for her across villages. Although she managed to escape several such attempts, she was finally arrested in 1932 and sentenced to life imprisonment. She was moved across various jails. In 1937, Jawaharlal Nehru met her in jail and gave her the title "Rani". She served her jail term till her release in 1947, when India finally became free.

Gaidinliu continued her good work for the upliftment of the Zeliangrong people after her release. She opposed the Naga National Council that wanted to break away from India after independence and insisted that the Zeliangrong people stay within India. She had to live underground for six years while fighting the Naga separatists and emerged in 1966 after reaching an agreement with the Indian government.

Gaidinliu was awarded the Tamrapatra Freedom Fighter Award in 1972 for her fight against the British. She was also bestowed with the Padma Bhushan in 1982 and received the Vivekananda Seva Award in 1983.

> Rani Gaidinliu was awarded the Tamrapatra, Padma Bhushan, Vivekananda Seva and Birsa Munda awards for her work.

She worked for the welfare of her people till her last breath and passed away in 1993 at the age of seventy-eight. She was awarded the Birsa Munda posthumously, and a postage stamp was released by the Indian government in her honour in 1996.

In 1996, a postage stamp was issued by the Indian government in Rani Gaidinliu's honour.

Activity

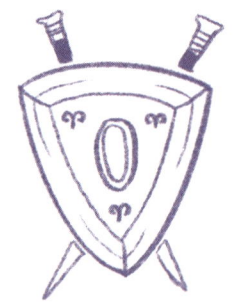

Find Your Purpose

Take a moment to think why a thirteen-year-old girl might choose danger over a comfortable life. Clearly, she valued something so much that it became the purpose of her life, a purpose so important that she was willing to sacrifice everything for it. Some of us may have to make such difficult choices in life. The one thing common to all leaders is the discovery of the ideas, values and goals which matter to them. Here is an exercise that will help you think about your goals and how you might reach them. Don't worry if you can't think of a big purpose yet! These things take time. Start practising with smaller goals. Perhaps you want to make sure your home segregates its waste. Or you want your family to start practising healthier eating habits. Or maybe you want your school to minimize the wastage of water and adopt water recycling. I encourage you to write down your goals in the activity sheet on the next page.

To download the activity PDF, scan this QR code:

MY PURPOSE

If I had a box of wishes, here are the three things I would like to do:

For myself I would
_____

For my friends I would
_____

For the world I would
_____

I AM A LEADER

If I lose my box of wishes I can still lead.

I am really good at
_____

What I need to achieve my dreams
_____

Words that describe me
_____

Velu Nachiyar

Was every little princess treated like a doll?
Sure, some royal girls were, but certainly not all;
In the case of brave and clever Velu Nachiyar
Childhood was spent getting ready for war.

Her father taught her many a battle skill
Combat rules and using weapons to kill;
Training in Horse riding and archery
Also, martial arts - Silambam and Valari.

And since warriors also negotiate peace,
Velu was taught to talk with much ease
In languages like French, Urdu and English
And she spoke many tongues with a flourish.

Velu was kept busy by this packed schedule
An only child, she was being trained to rule;
When the talented girl was good and ready
A suitable king was found for her wedding.

Velu's husband was respectable and kind
And a happier couple was hard to find;
**But he was killed by the East India Company
Queen Velu was left alone and had to flee.**

Her father's training had not gone waste
She vowed to fight back and made haste,
To reach out for help from one Hyder Ali
the mighty ruler of Mysore principality.

Hyder agreed and so did many others -
Tipu Sultan, Pillai and Marudhu brothers;
**After eight years of patient practice
Velu defeated the EIC's army with ease.**

But it took some unimaginable sacrifice
Before her kingdom's flag could again rise;
Velu found the EIC's ammunition depot
Commander Kuyili dealt it a body blow.

She knew that this was a suicide mission
But iron clad was the Velu army's conviction;
**Velu took charge of her dear kingdom and
In time passed it to her daughter's hand.**

People loved their Tamil warrior queen
Such valour and wisdom are seldom seen;
She set the bar, the standard so very high
She's earned the epithet Veeramangai.

Step 3: Initiative

Velu was proficient in many languages, including Urdu, English and French.

Raja Chellamuthu Vijayaragunatha Sethupathy and Rani Sakandhimuthal of the Ramnad kingdom in present-day Tamil Nadu were blessed with a baby girl on 3 January 1730. They named the child Velu. Since she was the couple's only child, her father insisted on bringing her up in a manner befitting a future monarch. He wanted her to be well equipped to handle matters of the state as well as the battlefield. Velu was trained in warfare, horse-riding and archery. She also learned Tamil martial arts like Silambam, which involves wielding a bamboo staff, and Valari, which uses a contraption like a boomerang. Velu was fluent in many languages including Urdu, English and French. This was a rare feat at a time when girls did not commonly receive education.

Velu married young, as was the custom of the time. Her husband, Muthu Vaduganatha Periyavudaya Thevar, was the King of Sivagangai. The couple had a daughter named Vellachi.

The King had to battle two enemies. The East India Company (EIC), which was already making inroads in India at the time, started to interfere with the state affairs. This was noticed and encouraged by the Nawab of Arcot, who coveted Sivagangai and tried to demand taxes on the kingdom. Since this demand had not been fulfilled by Velu's husband, the Nawab joined forces

Velu is the first Indian woman to have led her army to a win in a battle against the East India Company.

with the foreigners to try to defeat the King.

In 1772, Velu's husband was killed in a surprise attack by the combined forces of the EIC and the Nawab of Arcot. Velu had to flee the kingdom with her young daughter. After her husband's death, Velu lived in exile for eight years as a fugitive. She realized that she would not be able to win back her kingdom alone. She needed the help of strong friends and allies.

Velu's education in diplomacy and statecraft came in handy as she reached out to various Indian rulers for assistance. She succeeded in making alliances with strong rulers like Haider Ali, Nawab Tipu Sultan, the Marudhu brothers and Thandavarayan Pillai. She also approached rich merchants, who agreed to help her with funds. The external help, combined with her prowess

A postage stamp in Velu's honour was issued by the Indian Department of Posts in 2008.

> Velu raised an army during her exile and trained women fighters to take up prominent positions in the army.

as a trained fighter, made it possible for her to successfully raise an army. Notably, she trained women fighters and gave them prominent positions in her army.

When she felt the time was right, Velu marched to Sivagangai with her army. Despite their training and preparation, they were no match for the superior firepower of the EIC. Velu's trusted commander, a lady named Kuyili, made the ultimate sacrifice when she realized that the English ammunition depot would need to be destroyed for Velu's army to win. Legend has it that she entered the ammunition room and set herself ablaze, causing the entire stockpile of weapons to explode. This helped Velu to defeat the EIC's army, making her one of the very few Indians and the very first Indian woman to do so.

Velu thus regained her husband's kingdom and was crowned the Queen of Sivagangai in 1780. She ruled well for ten years before handing over the throne to Vellachi in 1790.

Velu passed away in 1796, but her memory lived on in the hearts and minds of Indians. In 2008, the Indian Department of Posts commemorated her by issuing a stamp in her honour. The city of Sivaganga has a memorial in her name as well as in the name of her beloved commander Kuyili. The ultimate honour for Velu comes from the common people, who remember her as "Veeramangai" or "brave woman".

Activity

Take Initiative

Have you wondered why some people are able to discover opportunities and create a path for themselves where others struggle? This quality of assuming responsibility for one's life is called initiative. One could have a lofty purpose but without initiative, action and energy, it cannot be fulfilled. Remember, we need to act to translate our purpose into reality.

Taking initiative comes from having a strong sense of confidence in our strengths and ability. We may not be able to run the world, but we can take charge of how we respond to it. Queen Velu was a self-starter and took charge of her own destiny without direction from anyone else. She chose to respond to the difficulties she faced after her husband's death without blaming her fate or drowning in worry. That's what leaders do. They do not wait for the world to give them a to-do list – they create their own agenda.

To download the activity PDF, scan this QR code:

Here is an "Initiative Dice" you can roll with a friend to prompt some thinking on how school students can display initiative in the many small activities that make up their daily life:

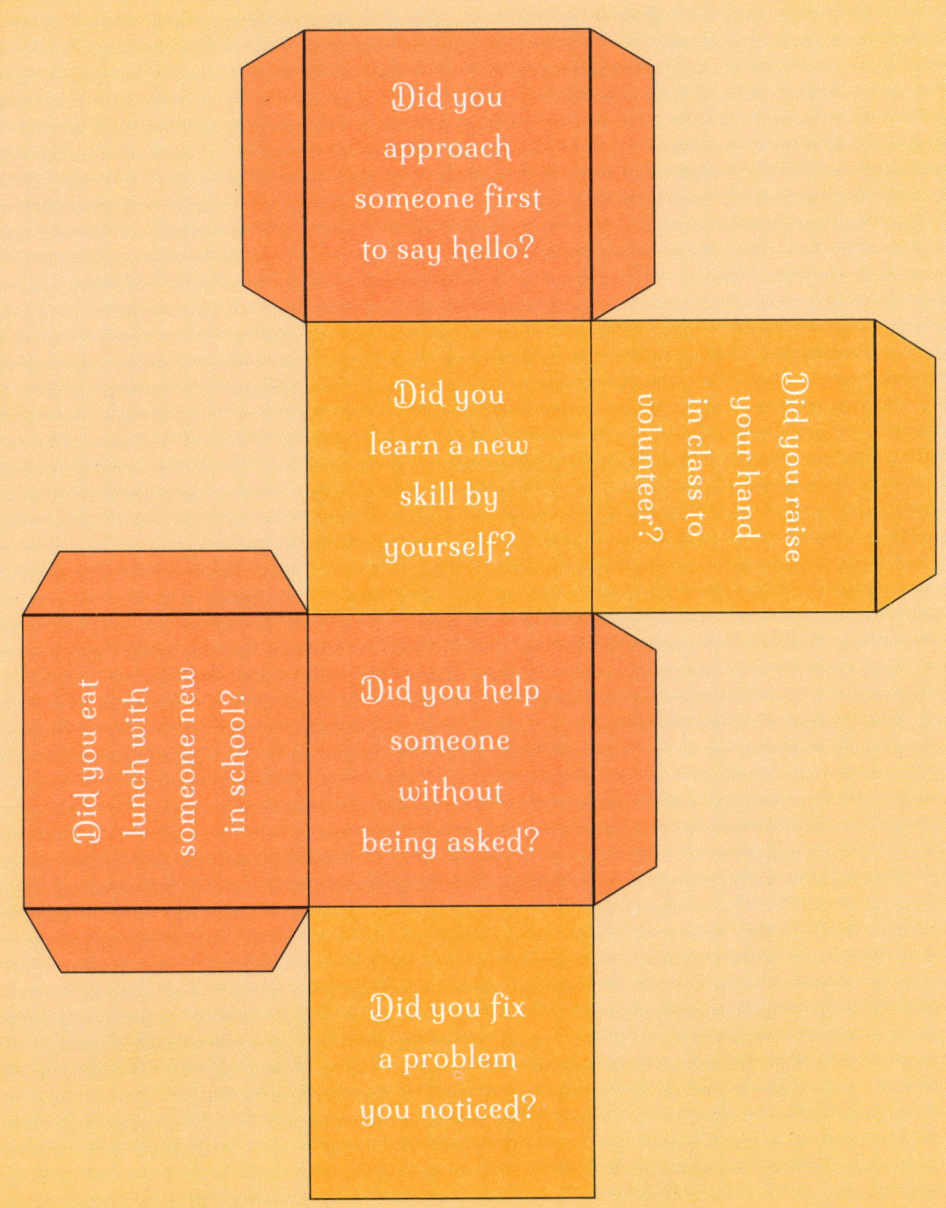

Abakka Chowta

Ancient India, as you may have heard
Was often compared to a golden bird;
Ships filled with lovely silks and spices
Sailed to Arabia for great prices.

Alas, this happiness came undone
With the first Portuguese ship and gun
That arrived uninvited upon Indian land.
With unabated greed, the visitors planned

To control all trade along the routes at sea;
Vasco da Gama's followers used their navy
To attack all Indian ships not paying a levy.

Now, there was a rather brave Queen
Abakka of Ullal, a leader strong and keen,

Who refused to buy the Portuguese permit,
And unlike the other kings, did not submit

To the foreign power and their devious ways;
She was fierce and her fire-tipped arrow
Terrified the enemy soldier to the marrow.

As the ships caught fire while still at sea,
The Portuguese jumped into the sea to flee.

Abakka made alliances with many a ruler
Who assured her help against the intruder;
She was just, simple and loved by one and all
Her loyal army was eager to answer her call.

She was good at administration and warfare
A queen with such great qualities was rare;
Yet there hid a man nursing a deep grouse
It was no stranger but her own spouse.

After years of fighting Abakka and facing defeat
This time the enemy had the advantage of deceit;
Abakka's estranged husband chose to guide
The Portuguese, and he betrayed his bride.

Abakka was captured and put in jail
Still, her courage did not flag nor fail;
She revolted and died fighting with pride
And tales of her glory are sung far and wide.

Step 4: Planning

Rani Abakka was an extraordinary warrior and an equally able stateswoman.

Did you know that during the "Age of Exploration" in the fifteenth century, India was so prosperous and played such an important role in international trade that finding a sea route to India was the dream of every European country? The first man to do so – Vasco da Gama – was from Portugal. Soon, the Portuguese established their fort in Calicut and began controlling all sea trade from India. Indian ships had to buy permits to sail, and the strong Portuguese navy was ordered to attack anyone who dared to trade without permission.

It was against this political backdrop that Abakka's story unfolded. She was the niece of the Chowta king Thirumala Raya III, who ruled a small kingdom called Ullal near present-day Mangalore. The Chowtas were Jain kings who were matrilineal. In matrilineal systems, inheritance of property as well as descent flows from mother to child. In accordance with this custom, Abakka became the heir apparent to the King.

Abakka displayed early signs of being brave and capable and was brought up to be a worthy successor. Her training focused on the two pillars considered important to rule – military technique and statecraft. Her weapon training made her an expert swordfighter and archer. She was taught military strategy as well as managing a

> Abakka was much loved by her people because she treated all religions as equal.

cavalry since soldiers travelled and fought on horseback. She learned state strategy and the art of diplomacy.

Abakka's uncle crowned her Queen and arranged her matrimonial alliance with Lakshmappa Bangaraja, the ruler of Banga near modern-day Mangalore. However, Abakka did not stay long with her husband and returned to Ullal with her children. Under her rule, Ullal prospered as a result of the flourishing spice trade through the sea route. This attracted the attention of the Portuguese, who asked her to pay a tribute to them to continue her trade unhindered.

Abakka rebuffed them and started reaching out to other regional rulers to forge strong alliances. She was able to win the trust and support of leaders like the Zamorin of Calicut and the King of Bidnur. She also cemented the loyalty of her people by welcoming people of all faiths and communities in her army and administration – Jains, Hindus and Muslims were well represented.

The Portuguese attacked Ullal in 1555, but Abakka's army was able to beat them successfully. They tried again in 1568, but once more Abakka was able to fight them back. And thus, Ullal stayed out of the grasp of the foreigners.

In 1570, Abakka made a new alliance with the Sultan of Bijapur in addition to the one

In 2015, the Indian Navy honoured Abakka's naval prowess by naming a patrol vessel after her.

Abakka's fire-tipped arrow

she had with the Zamorin. These two rulers too opposed the Portuguese and agreed to unite against them. By this time, the Portuguese were desperate to stop Abakka because her defiance was inspiring other rulers too. The tide turned against the Queen when her estranged husband was won over by the Portuguese and revealed secrets about Ullal and Abakka to the enemy.

In 1581, the Portuguese Viceroy of Goa, Anthony D' Noronha, led an armada of battleships to Ullal in a surprise pre-dawn attack. Abakka and her soldiers attacked the ships with flaming arrows and managed to burn down quite a few of them. However, Abakka was hurt in the fight and was captured and imprisoned. She rebelled in captivity too, and died brave and proud. Her legacy was carried on by her two daughters, who, like their mother, were strong and courageous.

Abakka's stories of valour are embedded in the folk culture of Dakshin Kannada. In 2003, the Indian Department of Posts issued a special stamp dedicated to Rani Abakka. In 2015, the Indian Navy acknowledged her naval prowess by naming a patrol vessel after her.

Heroines like Abakka live on in the memory of the people of their beloved country and attain immortality.

Activity

Plan

We read how leaders often have a larger purpose, a destination which guides their actions. However, this destination is not reached in a day. Smaller journeys add up to finally help them attain their dreams. These are the goals which we need to plan well.

One of Queen Abakka's many strengths was her ability to make sound plans with clear goals. The many treaties she successfully negotiated with powerful allies are examples of the goals she met to help her achieve her purpose to keep Ullal safe and prosperous. Now, think back to the purpose you identified for yourself after reading Gaidinliu Pamei's inspiring story. Here are some tools to help you plan your goals better. First, write down your goals. Then, pick the most important goal and dive deeper. Once you have written down your goals, share the list with someone who will hold you accountable for them. Your sibling or a friend would be perfect candidates.

To download the activity PDF, scan this QR code:

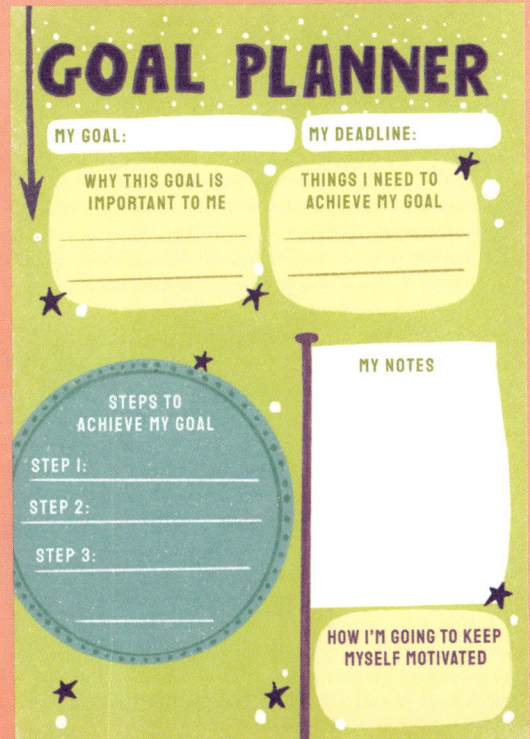

Ahilyabai Holkar

Ahilyabai was born in a household quite plain
Her father was no royal, just the village chieftain;
But while some queens are daughters of kings
Rare are the lucky ones for whom destiny sings.

Once as Ahilya was serving food at the temple
She was noticed by a man quite consequential;
The army commander of the Maratha Peshwa
Stopped to rest in her village as he travelled afar.

Quite impressed by the girl's character and piety
He got her married to his son in the year 1733;
The girl was taught well, but she was just eight
So, her wise mother-in-law decided to educate

This bright spark named Ahilya in the royal ways,
Lessons in politics and accounting filled her days;
Her married life was full of roses and sunshine
She was with her husband, even at the frontline.

Alas, this did not last as she lost him in a battle
A sad Ahilya got ready for sati, dazed and rattled;
Her father-in-law came to stop her just in time—
To allow this practice would have been a crime.

Ahilya was now trusted with great responsibility
She supported in affairs of the state and military;
The capture of Fort Gohad fell on her shoulders
As her father-in-law was away with his soldiers.

For 12 years she learned from that best among men
Then her son was crowned prince and she regent;
The prince died young, leaving Ahilya distraught
But she steeled herself, took charge and fought.

The pretenders swarmed around a woman alone
Their greedy, grubby hands just wanted the throne;
Crushing all opposition with her strength and tact
She declared herself Queen, quite matter-of-fact.

Thus, began the golden period of the Holkar dynasty
Of peace, prosperity, art, culture, trade and piety;
Her spirituality was her compass, her guiding light
Ahilya's flame burns on in our nation, ever so bright.

Step 5: Communication

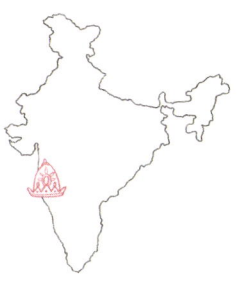

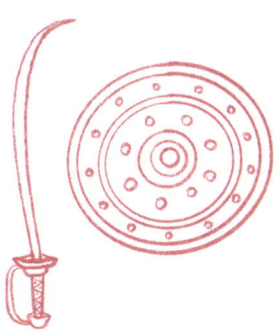

When Ahilya lost her husband in battle, she wanted to commit sati. But her father-in-law stopped her and trained her in military strategy.

Every so often, one comes across people so extraordinary, that one can only wonder at the breadth of their accomplishments. Ahilyabai Holkar is one such legend who is a notch above all because of the impact she created in her thirty years of rule. What makes her story even more impressive is the fact that she was not born into a royal family and were it not for a quirk of fate, she would probably have led a simple village life.

On 31 May 1725, the village headman of Chaundi village near present-day Ahmednagar in Maharashtra welcomed a baby girl. She was named Ahilya, and unlike the prevalent customs of the time, she was encouraged to read and write.

One day, Ahilya was helping out at an event at the local temple, where food was being served to the needy. As luck would have it, she caught the attention of a gentleman named Malhar Rao Holkar, who thought she displayed superlative character and devotion to the needy. Even though Ahilya was just eight, he decided she was the right bride for his son. In those days, it was customary for girls to be married quite young, so this was not unusual.

The Holkars were influential people – Malhar Rao was a powerful leader in the Malwa region and held the key position of Commander in the Maratha Peshwa's army. Ahilya was thus married into a prominent family with ties to the Maratha royalty.

Ahilya's kind mother-in-law personally oversaw her upbringing and education. She was groomed to understand how to run the administration of a state. She was also imparted a strong set of values. She routinely accompanied her husband Khanderao on his military campaigns.

After the demise of her husband in 1754, a grief-stricken Ahilya tried to commit sati in accordance with the prevalent custom at the time. Her father-in-law stopped her just in time. He gave her military training, and relied on her to carry out military campaigns when he was occupied elsewhere.

Malhar Rao died in 1766, twelve years after the death of his son. Following this, his grandson became the ruler of Indore under Ahilya's supervision. However, he too died within a few months of becoming King. Ahilya stepped up to take charge of the beloved land of her in-laws. She faced threats and open hostility from other claimants to the throne, who saw her as a weak woman without anyone to help her. However, her diplomacy and military prowess won her the support of other rulers, and she was soon able to quell all opposition.

The next thirty years of Ahilya's rule transformed her kingdom into a very prosperous and culturally advanced region.

> The arts and textiles flourished under Ahilyabai's patronage. The popular Maheshwari sari is named after Ahilya's capital city of Maheshwar.

Ahilyabai worked for the betterment of pilgrimage sites across her kingdom and even beyond.

Her capital city was Maheshwar, a city on the banks of the river Narmada. The arts and textiles developed under her patronage, and the popular Maheshwari saris were named after her capital. The nearby village of Indore too was developed into a major city.

One of Ahilyabai's long-lasting legacies is the betterment she brought about at pilgrimage centres across India. Temples, river ghats, rest houses and wells and other water bodies were developed for the common man in her kingdom and beyond.

One can only marvel at the impact of her good governance and far-sighted vision. She worked tirelessly to make her people's lives better till the end of her days. Although she passed away at the age of seventy, she lives on in the many songs and stories that people still share about their philosopher queen.

Statue of Ahilyabai Holkar in Maheshwar

Activity

Communicate

Once a leader like Queen Ahilyabai has decided on an ambitious purpose and planned her goals, how does she make sure everyone around her understands what she is trying to achieve? How does she inspire and motivate people to join her and support her cause? The answer, of course, is through communication. Think of a leader you admire. They are probably good at expressing their thoughts – most good leaders have learned to speak and write well. They also make the effort to listen carefully when someone is talking to them. Let's brush up our communication skills.

To download the activity PDF, scan this QR code:

First, let's learn to listen better with whole body listening.

Have you wondered how to convey your message so that your audience understands you perfectly, without any mistakes? Well, here are the 7 Cs of communication which you can refer to each time you have to say something really important:

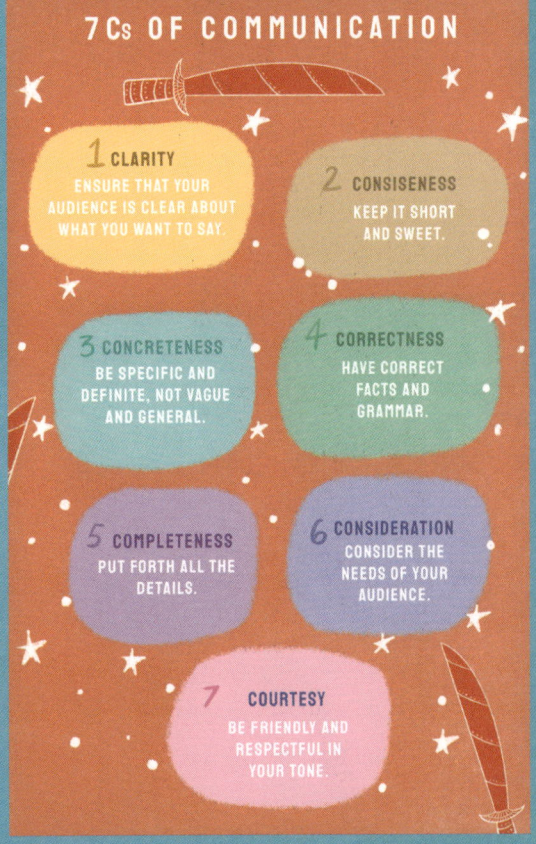

Now that you have learned to communicate effectively, let's put it to the test! Make a video about your favourite queen and use the 7 Cs of communication to talk about what makes her your favourite.
Post the video with the hashtag #gutsygirls to share it with other young readers. Also try to apply your learnings: How many of the 7 Cs were you able to use? What form of communication was this?

Keladi Chennamma

Have you seen grandma's old photographs?
Some black and white, others blurry perhaps;
Like fleeting clips from a half-forgotten cinema
Such is the story of Queen Keladi Chennamma.

We don't have a written history with all details
But on examining records and hearing old tales,
We can declare she was amazing in many ways
And earned Keladi Kingdom everlasting praise.

Chennamma was born to a trader, a Lingayata
And was married to King Somashekara Nayaka;
But, widowed young, she became the ruler
She exhibited many rare virtues and used her
Bravery and foresight to reign well and long
For twenty-five years she kept Keladi strong.

When Shivaji's son requested her for refuge
She agreed knowing well the waiting deluge,

Of Emperor Aurangzeb's terrible punishment
That made every king quake in fear and relent;
When the Mughal attack on Keladi took place
Chennamma fearlessly led her forces to face.

Her military strength and planning won the day
And this time Aurangzeb could not go "hurray";
A treaty was drawn up after the attack failed
Shivaji's son was saved and justice prevailed.

Chennamma assured him safety and freedom
She also ensured that he got a generous sum;
While this historic event was applauded by all
She did kind gestures for people big and small.

Chennamma of Keladi, is such a rare treasure
She set a high standard beyond any measure.

Step 6: Empathy

Chennamma was the daughter of a merchant and did not have any royal connection before her marriage to the King of Keladi.

Sometimes, a single act of courage by a fearless leader can shine on like the sun, providing warmth and inspiration for centuries after they're gone. **Keladi Chennamma is one such leader who dared to take on the scariest, strongest and most unforgiving opponents and emerged victorious.** And she did this not to save herself, but to defend someone else who had requested her protection.

We turn our time machine to the seventeenth century as we fly down to the town of Keladi in present-day Shimoga district of Karnataka. Today, this town is a tourist destination because of its famous Rameshwara temple. Back in the day, the Nayaka dynasty lived and ruled here.

Chennamma was born in the house of a rich merchant, but destiny had other plans for her. She was married off to the King of Keladi, Somashekara Nayaka I, and moved into the royal palace as his queen in 1663. She adapted well to her new role and responsibilities. The King was keen to have a son but passed away under mysterious circumstances before his dream could come true.

Young Chennamma was left alone amidst ministers and relatives who coveted the throne. However, she emerged victorious in the palace intrigues and declared herself the Queen. She consolidated her power over time and defended Keladi from attacks by neighbouring states that wanted to try their luck against a woman ruler.

As Chennamma ably administered her kingdom, fate presented her with a unique test of bravery. Rajaram, the son of Shivaji, was on the run as the army of the Mughal emperor Aurangzeb followed him in hot pursuit. He requested permission from Chennamma to pass through her kingdom as he transited to a safe place.

Now, this was not an easy request to accept. Aurangzeb was extremely strong and rather quick to get angry. The Marathas were his bitter enemies, so giving shelter to Rajaram would be very dangerous. Every other kingdom had turned down Rajaram's request already, since no one wanted to incur Aurangzeb's wrath. The small kingdom of Keladi was no match for the mighty Mughals, and the Queen did not want the common man to suffer in the event of a war.

Yet Chennamma could not decline the plea of the Maratha heir and prepared for the retribution that was sure to arrive. When the Mughal army clashed with her forces, Chennamma did not flinch. Her brave forces fought well. The Mughal army was also besieged by heavy rain and illness. They discovered that Rajaram had already fled Keladi and hence decided to withdraw after signing a treaty with Chennamma. This made Chennamma one of the few Indian rulers to successfully defeat Aurangzeb.

Chennamma once provided shelter and protection to Shivaji's son, Rajaram Bhosle, against the mighty Mughals.

Chennamma's life has inspired several TV series and works of fiction.

Chennamma was a great leader in times of peace as well. She ruled for twenty-five years and ensured peace and prosperity in her kingdom. After her death, her close relative and adopted son, Basavappa Nayaka, took over the reins.

Keladi Chennamma is remembered fondly, and her life has inspired several television series and stories. Channagiri, a town in Karnataka, is named after her.

Activity

Be Empathetic

What does the word empathy mean and why is it important for a leader? Often, a leader will meet people who have opinions different from themself. How should a leader react in such a situation? By walking a mile in the other person's shoes. Not literally, of course. The expression means that a leader should try to understand the other person's point of view and what they are feeling. Queen Chennamma displayed this quality when she understood the situation Shivaji's son faced when he was on the run from a very strong enemy. Now, try to think of someone you know who is different from you in their thinking, race, gender, age or some other characteristic. Think about a time that you put yourself in their shoes. What happened? What did you do? In the shoe on the facing page, write what you learned or how you felt upon behaving with empathy. Try to complete the exercise keeping them in mind.

To download the activity PDF, scan this QR code:

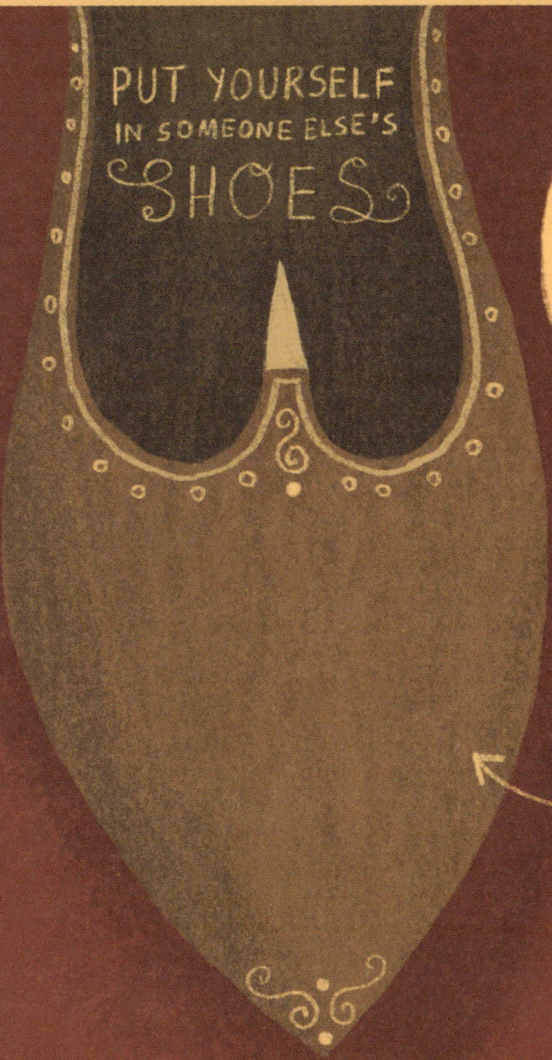

PUT YOURSELF IN SOMEONE ELSE'S SHOES

THIS SHOE BELONGS TO
_____
_____

I LISTEN TO UNDERSTAND OTHERS

Use words or pictures to describe an incident where you put yourself in someone else's shoes.

A GOOD LEADER listens, learns and understands before responding.

A GOOD LEADER works to solve problems in an unbiased way.

Mai Bhago

We are now going to Punjab – the land of the five rivers
With its tales of bravery that give us thrills and shivers;
The story you'll hear next has not been told too often
Its glory and power will make the hardest heart soften.

A spiritual Sikh family was blessed with an only girl child
They declared her a blessed one and truly fortune smiled;
She had many names – first Bhag Bhari, then Bhag Kaur
Finally came Mai Bhago – her moniker from one and all.

These were the decades when the newly made religion
Became the target of Aurangzeb's ruthless persecution;
Mai Bhago grew up hearing tales of sacrifice and of war
And learned that some causes were worth fighting for.

Her family was surprisingly emancipated and modern
And trained Mai Bhago to take the road less trodden;
While the other women only lived for home and hearth
Our girl was taught the skills to be a warrior from birth.

She met Guru Gobind Singh – the Holy One, The Source
And wanted to stay back and train to join the Sikh force;
Since her plan to join male soldiers faced disparage
She reluctantly settled for her marriage.

When Guru Gobind Singh was attacked by the Mughals
His last forty men abandoned the Guru and his struggles;
Mai Bhago heard this, and their cowardice made her livid
She persuaded them to go back and stop being so timid.

All forty were martyred when Aurangzeb's forces attacked
She lost her brothers and husband with her life barely intact;
Still, her timely intervention had saved her Guru and her faith.

This saint-warrior became the Guru's first female bodyguard
And lived to a ripe old age having broken every single record.

Step 7: Team Play

This is a story of such incredible heroism and brazen bravery that we need to begin at the end. A lady successfully led forty men into battle against a formidable Mughal army of ten thousand men. Knowing fully well that there was no chance of surviving the fearsome odds, she rallied her men to defend their Guru. This act of resistance was able to save the young Sikh religion from Aurangzeb's deadly attack.

Who was this lady? How could she overcome her fear? And why did the men obey her? Why did they accept her as their leader even in the face of death?

The story begins in Punjab in 1666 in the home of a prominent family in the village of Jhabal Kalan near present-day Amritsar. The family were delighted at the birth of a baby girl after being blessed with boys earlier. They called her "Bhag Kaur" or the lucky one. She was later also called Mata Bhag Kaur or Mai Bhago as a mark of respect.

> Mai Bhago, the only girl in a family with male children, was given military training alongside her brothers.

Bhag Kaur was born at a time and in a place that shaped her strong character and iron will. Her father, Bhai Mallo Shah, was a Sikh landowner who had served in the army of Guru Hargobind, and the family often travelled to meet Guru Gobind Singh in Anandpur. Along with her brothers, little Bhag Kaur also received military training. This was quite unique for the time and reflected the Sikh teaching of treating people equally irrespective of gender or class. In fact, young Bhag Kaur wanted to join the

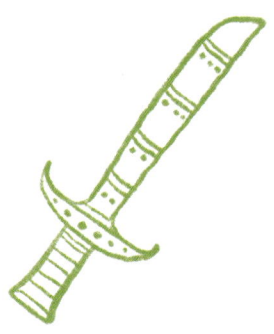

Mai Bhago motivated forty men who had abandoned Guru Gobind Singh to return to fight against Aurangzeb's Mughal army.

Sikh army herself, but since there were very few women like her, the army did not have a women's unit at that time.

Instead, Mai Bhago got married to Bhai Nidhan Singh on her parents' suggestion. She could have chosen to lead a life of quiet domestic bliss, like most women in that era were expected to. However, she was keenly aware of the danger her people and way of life faced from the Mughal emperor Aurangzeb. He viewed the rise of the Sikh religion as a threat to his power and was determined to crush it.

Aurangzeb sent his army to surround Anandpur Sahib to capture Guru Gobind Singh. The siege lasted months and food supplies started running out, causing great distress to the followers of the Guru. At this time, forty Sikh followers of the Guru deserted him and escaped to freedom.

Mai Bhago was deeply unhappy at the thought that the Guru had been left alone at this time of danger. Displaying impressive leadership, she spoke to the deserters about their betrayal and urged them to go back. The forty men were embarrassed by their weakness and decided to follow Mai Bhago back to their Guru and make amends by asking for his forgiveness.

By now, the Guru had left the fort with his remaining forces, the Mughal army at their heels in hot pursuit. Mai Bhago and the forty men she was leading arrived at the village of Khidrana to meet the Guru. The Mughal

Mai Bhago's life provides inspiring lessons to us all on leadership, bravery and service to the community.

army too arrived here and tried to make their way to a pool which happened to be the only source of water in the area. In the legendary battle that took place, the forty Sikhs fought the full might of the Mughals even as they knew that death was certain. Mai Bhago lost her loved ones in the battle and was herself injured. Luckily, the Mughal army retreated as soon as they saw that the pool was dry.

The forty men, who had initially deserted their Guru and ultimately sacrificed their lives, are immortalized as the Chali Mukte or the Forty Immortal Ones. The Guru looked after the injured Mai Bhago, who expressed a desire to join his team of bodyguards. This request was accepted, and she lived and travelled with the Guru until his death in Nanded.

After the Guru's death, Mai Bhago travelled further and settled down at a place called Janwada near the town of Bidar in Karnataka. She lived to a ripe old age, preaching the Guru's teachings and meditation to followers.

Mai Bhago's hut is now converted into a gurdwara and continues to serve the community.

Activity

Be a Team Player

Mai Bhago was able to successfully lead forty reluctant and fearful men into battle against the mighty Mughal army. The men must have known that they did not stand much of a chance against Aurangzeb's forces. And yet, they chose to follow Mai Bhago in battle. How did this happen? The answer is Mai Bhago's unparalleled leadership, ability to be a team player and inspire the men towards a shared purpose.

A good leader is able to become a part of their team and treat each and every member as an equal. They not only work in harmony with others but are also willing to learn from them. Why do you think these qualities are important? Share your thoughts in the activity sheet.

To download the activity PDF, scan this QR code:

TEAM PLAY

TEAM
A GROUP OF PEOPLE WORKING TOGETHER TOWARDS A COMMON GOAL

Together Everyone Achieves More

COOPERATION
CHOOSING TO WORK WELL WITH OTHERS

TEAM PLAY IS IMPORTANT BECAUSE:

USE WORDS OR PICTURES TO SHARE AN EXAMPLE OF SOMETHING YOU ACHIEVED AS PART OF A TEAM.

Rani Lakshmibai

When the day is done, the lights turn soft and dreamland is calling
We long to read something special, a tale evergreen and enthralling;
Something that tickles hearts and minds, and sets imagination ablaze
Something with songs, books, poems, plays and movies in its praise.

What can we add to what's been said? Well, here's our humble try -
Let's gather close to hear once more the legend of Rani Lakshmibai;
Varanasi was the city where baby Manikarnika let out her first cry
Her family pampered her, she was the apple of their eye.

She lost her mother young, and was brought up by her dear father
He worked for the Peshwa who too had a deep fondness for her;
Since Manikarnika was brought up with the boys from royalty
She was trained in fighting wars and commanding armies easily.

She grew up to be brave and beautiful and married a Maharaja
And was renamed "Lakshmibai" in a tradition uniquely Maratha;
They soon had a baby boy, but he passed away very young
The parents were heartbroken, the pain too deeply stung.

Soon after, the Maharaja also died, leaving Jhansi in her care
But before he passed away, he adopted a young boy as his heir;
Enter the British with the "Doctrine of Lapse" and their games sly
They claimed to own Jhansi, denying the rights of the young boy.

At first Queen Lakshmibai tried to use reason and legal recourse
The British did not listen so she knew she had to use force;
"I will not surrender my Jhansi" was her unforgettable battle cry
As she took on the foreign occupants who were bleeding India dry.

She was not alone, for in the year 1857 the spark was truly lit
And the Indians finally rose up to fight against the occupying Brits;
On the day of the final battle, Lakshmibai's bravery was on display
When defeat seemed imminent, she escaped to fight another day.

She strapped her son to her body, her loyal Badal neighed closeby
Badal plunged from the fort wall, knowing fully well he might die;
Bidding him a quick goodbye the Queen walked instead of riding
Alas, she did not make it far before she was caught in firefighting.

She fought well but eventually was shot and injured by the enemy,
She lives on still, brave and free, in the nation's collective memory.

Step 8: Resilience

Rani Lakshmibai loved horses. Of those she owned, Badal was her favourite and sacrificed his own life to help her escape the British army.

Rani Lakshmibai. It's a name synonymous with bravery, sacrifice and leadership. In fact, there have been so many stories, plays, poems, books and movies on her that fact and fiction sometimes blend to create an almost mythical saga of unmatched proportions.

Let's begin at the beginning of her story. It was the nineteenth day of November when a young Maratha couple living in Varanasi welcomed their daughter into this world. They named her Manikarnika, and affectionately called her Manu.

Manu's mother died when she was young. Her father, Moropant Tambe, worked for Peshwa Baji Rao II near modern-day Kanpur. The Peshwa noticed the energy and intelligence of young Manu and became fond of the child. Unlike the other girls of her time, Manu received the education reserved for young boys in the Peshwa's court. This included warfare, study of religious texts and sports like fencing and shooting. She became proficient at horse riding and sword fighting. This early training shaped her mind and body, and she became ready to embrace her destiny as a brave warrior.

In May 1842, when she was fourteen, Manu was married off to the Maharaja of Jhansi, Gangadhar Rao. In keeping with the family tradition, she was given a new name – Lakshmibai – after the wedding. Unfortunately, the couple's baby son died of illness, and soon Lakshmibai's husband too

To honour Rani Lakshmibai, the Indian National Army named their women's unit after her – the Rani of Jhansi Regiment.

passed away, passing on the reigns to his wife. However, before his death in November 1853, the Maharaja adopted a male child and named him Damodar Rao. He wanted to make sure that Jhansi would continue to be ruled well with Rani Lakshmibai on the throne while the boy grew into adulthood.

However, the then British governor general of India, Lord Dalhousie, did not recognize the boy as the rightful heir and used a policy called the Doctrine of Lapse to annex Jhansi. He posted an agent of the East India Company to manage Jhansi and asked the Rani to move out of her fort.

Rani Lakshmibai bided her time. She continued to rally her loyal supporters, both civilians and soldiers, and maintained a disciplined and active lifestyle. After the First War of Independence in 1857, she was proclaimed Queen by Indian freedom fighters who attacked the British army that had captured the fort of Jhansi.

Once back on the throne, Rani Lakshmibai strengthened the defence of the fort in

Rani Lakshmibai's former residence has been converted to a museum and is now known as Rani Mahal. Archaeological artworks and sculptures dating back to the ninth and twelfth centuries as well as weapons used by the Rani during the mutiny of 1857 can be found here.

anticipation of a British attack, which came in 1858 when the British army, led by Sir Hugh Rose, surrounded her fort on 23 March. The dauntless Rani fought fiercely. When it became clear that the British forces would enter the fort, she tied her adopted son to her back and jumped down from a wall on the back of her trusted horse Badal. She and her son escaped unhurt, but Badal died in the fall.

Rani Lakshmibai led her troops in many successful battles, motivating them with her bravery, until she finally died in a battle on the outskirts of Gwalior in June 1858. Over the years, the stories of her valour have become most beloved and popular, and her name is now synonymous with exemplary courage and patriotism.

Numerous educational institutions in India and even a marine national park in Andaman and Nicobar Islands are named after the much-loved Rani of Jhansi.

The seal of Rani Lakshmibai of Jhansi

Activity

Be Resilient

Rani Lakshmibai had a quality that all great leaders use to deal with the inevitable setbacks everyone faces in their journeys – resilience. It is a fancy word to describe the ability to bounce back after facing failure. If leaders give up on their purpose at the first sign of struggle, they will never be able to turn their dreams into reality.

How can you build resilience? Here are six bouncy balls that you can use to get better at this game. Together, they will help you recover to fight another day!

To download the activity PDF, scan this QR code:

Here's a simple way to help you or your friend bounce back when you hit a wall and need some cheering up. Carefully cut out both circles and join them together at the centre using a pin. Rotate the orange circle and pick the option you like.

Begum Hazrat Mahal

Get aboard dear reader, we are off on an adventure
As a young girl starts life with the odds against her;
This innocent child from Faizabad near Lucknow
Had the weight of the world on her furrowed brow.

For her own parents had dealt her the cruellest blow
They traded her for money, she had family no more;
Muhammedi Khanum took to a profession forbidden
Unprotected and all alone, she became a courtesan.

Yet the young lady knew all days would not be the same
It's not the cards you hold, but how you play the game;
Our girl's face was her fortune, but she was also bright
An attendant at the Royal Harem, she proved just right.

Her work was appreciated, and she was soon promoted;
In fact, the last King of Awadh, Wajid Ali, noted
her charm, personality and her beauty on which he doted.

He made her "Begum" and when she had their son
He made her "Hazrat Mahal", a transformation was done;
Her only son, Birjis Qadr, became the apple of her eye
Her days were filled with joy, the years just slipped by.

Unnoticed by them though, the world was changing fast
The British wanted Awadh, the sunny skies grew overcast;
Wajid Ali was exiled and left Hazrat and Birjis in Lucknow
Planning to be back soon, for how was he to know?

Never again would he by his loved ones be seen
Birjis took to the throne and Hazrat became Queen;
The British called the Indian Rebellion of 1857 a mutiny
But Hazrat and her forces backed the Indian rebels fully.

As the leader of the uprising, she was strong and wise
She knew freedom for all Indians was a worthy prize;
Joining her in fight were Nana Sahab and Maulvi Shah
For a while it seemed they would have the last hurrah.

Alas, the British troops defeated the Indian rebels finally
They offered Hazrat peace and even money in a treaty;
She did not trust the British and refused their mercy
She left with her family to Nepal, choosing to live free.

This leader of freedom fighters was India's true daughter
Neither British money nor comfort could have bought her;
Hazrat Mahal started her journey in poverty as a slave
But she left the world an immortal - a leader so brave.

Step 9: Self-care

Begum Hazrat Mahal was trained in dance, drama, music, court etiquette and politics at Wajid Ali Shah's Parikhana.

You may have come across the word "leadership" quite often, but what does it really mean? Every one of us can be a leader. Since there is no cookie cutter which can be used to "cut out" perfectly shaped leaders, they come in many different types of personalities.

Let's go to the grand city of Lucknow to discover a rather unlikely story of leadership.

A very poor slave had to make the heartbreaking decision that no parent should have to - selling off his own child to agents who supplied slaves to the royal establishment. The child, named Muhammedi Khanum, was born in Faizabad in 1820 in the erstwhile state of Awadh.

While this was the worst start to her life, Lucknow was quite the cultural hotspot at the time, with royal patronage for artists of all kinds. The King of Awadh, Wajid Ali Shah, was one of the most generous supporters of Indian fine arts. He ran a famous school of sorts, called Parikhana (or the abode of fairies), where experts taught dance, drama and music to young girls.

Young Muhammedi was trained in the arts here and picked up court etiquette and an awareness of politics too. She was appreciated by the King, who married her and gave her the title of Hazrat Mahal as a mark of respect once she had a son. The slave girl was now one of his favourite

Begum Hazrat Mahal actively participated in the First War of Indian Independence in 1857, leading rebels in their armed fight against the British.

queens, and her son, Birjis Qadr, was brought up with the amenities and education befitting a young prince.

However, this stable and happy world came crashing down when Wajid Ali was exiled to Calcutta by the British in 1856. He left with his queens and servants for what he expected to be a temporary stay. Hazrat Mahal chose to stay back in Lucknow with Birjis. She had witnessed the intrigue and turmoil that the British were fostering in the Indian masses and was resolutely against the destruction of Indian places of worship by the foreign forces.

In 1857, when the Indian troops stood up in an uprising against the British, Hazrat Mahal not only supported them, but led them from the front. She installed her son on the throne and led the rebel forces in their armed fight. She became a respected rallying force behind whom Indians from various parts of the country united. She started by working with the renowned freedom fighter Nana Saheb. Later, she joined forces with the Maulavi of Faizabad when his forces launched an attack on Shahjahanpur. She met freedom fighters and issued directions and proclamations to the forces. She is also known to have mounted an elephant to personally participate in a battle.

After some initial success, the rebel forces were weakened when the British regrouped and attacked again. Soon, most of Lucknow

> Begum Hazrat Mahal was made an offer of peace by the British, which would have ensured her safety and financial stability. She rejected it.

was recaptured by the British, and they started winning back most of the Awadh region. Begum Hazrat Mahal was faced with a choice – surrender to the British or escape to fight another day. She was made a peace offer which, if she had accepted, would have assured her safety and enough riches to live comfortably. However, she rejected the offer. She did not want to live according to the terms dictated by the enemy. Also, she did not trust the British since she had seen enough examples of their betrayal, especially with her husband.

Begum Hazrat Mahal chose to escape to Nepal and lived there with her son till her death in 1879. She cherished her freedom and worked for India's independence from British rule till the very end. She is remembered with great respect – a stamp was issued in her honour by the Indian government on 10 May 1984. The government also established a Begum Hazrat Mahal National Scholarship for meritorious girls belonging to minority communities.

Activity

Practise Self-Care

Being a leader can be hard, hard work! Besides looking out for and supporting others, leaders must look after themselves too, and take responsibility for their own wellness and happiness. A tired and sad person can hardly be expected to have the energy to achieve their goals and help others do the same. Remember what the flight attendant tells you on an aircraft? Put your own oxygen mask on first before you aid someone else in case of an emergency.

To download the activity PDF, scan this QR code:

← MOST VALUABLE PERSON

Your Photo

A Leader takes care of their health.

A Leader is their own friend.

A Leader knows that we make mistakes and forgives themself and others.

I'm really good at

_____
_____
_____

I'm special because

_____
_____

I deserve love, care and kindness.

SELF-CARE
· CHECKLIST ·

- ☐ Restful sleep
- ☐ Healthy and tasty food
- ☐ Your favourite physical sport
- ☐ Enough water through the day
- ☐ A short walk in the sun
- ☐ Dancing to your favourite songs
- ☐ A chat with a good friend
- ☐ Playing with a pet
- ☐ My favourite thing 1
- ☐ My favourite thing 2

Rani Durgavati

Now we hop over to the North Indian state of U.P.
'Twas 1524, folk were celebrating the days of Navratri;
The king was in his castle when he got the good news
He'd had a daughter, and her name he must choose.

She was born on Durgashtami so she was called Durgavati
And this child of the Rajputs was trained to fight valiantly;
She grew up accomplished in all things martial and royal
At eighteen she wedded a king, trading vows to be loyal.

Gondwana, in the heart of India, was her new homeland
Durgavati felt welcomed by Dalpat, who was a kind man;
It was a political alliance, as was common among royalty
Everyone celebrated soon when Durgavati had a baby.

They named him Vir Narayan – the Brave One,
True to his name, the prince was second to none;
Unfortunately, he lost his father at the tender age of five
Durgavati became the Queen, Gondwana had to thrive.

She was an able ruler, her training was put to good use
There was trade, peace and people had enough produce;
She moved her capital to a new fort with strategic intent
And managed an army which had man, horse and elephant.

Her first test came soon when Baz Bahudur came to attack
Our brave warrior fought him and sent him scurrying back;
She kept winning wars and kept her kingdom protected
Art, trade and music thrived, many buildings were erected.

But an ill wind was blowing from Delhi – the Mughals had arrived
Their army attacked her many times, yet Durgavati survived;
In the last war Vir Narayan was hurt and sent to a safe place
The Queen was shot too and knew it was the end of the race.

Not wanting to be captured, she fought on even as she bled
And Indians bow in reverence to this fearless leader who led.

Step 10: Leadership

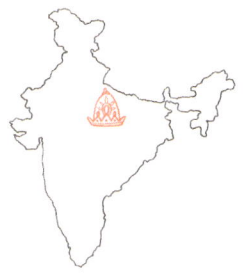

Under Rani Durgavati's charge, Gondwana prospered, and art, music and religion flourished in the region.

Do you know what your name means? In India, parents often choose names for their children based on the qualities they hope their child will display. Young Durgavati was named after Goddess Durga, and she lived up to her name by displaying exemplary bravery in her life.

Although Durgavati was born at a time when girls were expected to limit themselves to domestic tasks, our princess was brought up with an education any prince would be lucky to get. She was especially gifted at all skills needed to become a good warrior. In 1542, when she turned eighteen, she got married to King Dalpat Shah of Gondwana, who was quite an accomplished fighter himself. Although it was intended as an alliance between two prominent kingdoms, it was also a happy marriage.

Durgavati gave birth to a son whom they named Vir Narayan. Unfortunately, Durgavati lost her husband when her son was just five years old. A deep grief took over her. Since her son was very young, her husband's ministers requested her to take charge of the kingdom.

Durgavati was no stranger to administration of the kingdom since her husband had kept her involved right from the beginning. She was also suitably aided by loyal ministers who wanted Gondwana to stay safe and protected. She decided to leave her old capital at Singorgarh and moved to a fort in

> Rani Durgavati's forces defeated Baz Bahadur's army so resoundingly that he never dared to look at her kingdom again.

the Satpura hills named Chauragarh, which was considered a better location strategically in case of a battle.

Rani Durgavati's first challenge was Baz Bahadur's attack on the kingdom.. The heroic Queen defeated the army of the intruders so decisively that he never dared to look at her kingdom again. Her able leadership extended off the battlefield as well. Under her charge, the people prospered, and art, music and religion flourished. She made sure that dams, water tanks and temples were built for the benefit of the common people. She was loved and respected and, for a while, it seemed that the happy days would last forever.

However, the riches of the Gondwana kingdom attracted the attention of other kings, who were jealous. Baz Bahadur was defeated by Akbar's forces, and Queen Durgavati became an immediate neighbour of the Mughals, whose policy was to expand their rule. Gondwana was no exception.

When the Mughal General Asaf Khan attacked them, the Queen was advised to surrender. The Mughal army was huge, and the Gondwana army would be no match for it. But she chose to fight because she believed it was the more honourable option.

When the battle took place, Rani Durgavati's forces were able to repulse the attack initially. When night fell, the Queen wanted

Rani Durgavati bravely fought the Mughals and chose to end her own life to avoid capture and mistreatment at their hands.

to continue the offensive, but her generals suggested they wait till the morning. As it turned out, Queen Durgavati's instinct was right. The Mughal forces received reinforcements in the night and the tide had turned by morning. Vir Narayan retired hurt and had to be moved to a hiding place. The Queen rode out on her elephant to fight with a depleted band of soldiers. She suffered two arrow shots and knew that defeat was imminent. Instead of suffering the ignominy of being captured and mistreated by the Mughals, the Queen chose to end her life, ensuring her pride and dignity remained intact till the end.

Today, women and men alike can only marvel at the fiercely brave leader who defied all gender norms of her times to lead with courage, honour and fortitude. There have been gestures of respect for Rani Durgavati in recent times. The University of Jabalpur was renamed the Rani Durgavati Vishwavidyalaya in her memory. A stamp was issued in her name by the Indian government.

Rani Durgavati of Gondwana

Activity

Become an Effective Leader

Now that we have seen examples of inspiring leaders with different personalities across various regions and ages, you will find it easy to solve the leadership puzzle on this page. Remember, effective leadership requires a combination of all the qualities we have discussed so far in the book. Your leadership style will be as unique as you are. It will be a combination of *your* personality and *your* purpose and will evolve with time. It's a marathon, not a sprint. Be patient, be kind and above all, enjoy the journey.

To download the activity PDF, scan this QR code:

LEADERSHIP PUZZLE

```
          ADS
        FNBKFJHG
      SFOSEJGNERLKV
     ASHJANLDKASLFKNAASKA
    MJKJHASADASFLKAWLRFWOJWI
    LEFDAHDKCNASWNKJJASZKCJSZ
    ADGAWUHRWNACDUIEHRWRERVDS
    YFLWIRLJESFIOHWADJNASKDFJN
    OKPJLTFHAYUSGDWBJUAHSUEHKS
    NBFIHIUGEHSJDOIKJCAOHSAKJNC
    YRHTUDIUFJDSIUHRAJKWHBDSSD
     OIPOUKLNCVKJSBDWJENBWJKBD
     DTUYRHIHNDVUBWUHDEKJWSB
      UHTKNFKJHVUWEBDJHWBSXJ
      WQQWMLKVDCVNSOREIEREK
       BBDOIJFWIJDAQEWLFEKA
        POPSKFLJSLKHFCNDW
         TEWAKWPSKAPCJS
           IUJVFNBDGI
             AWEUS
              IEU
```

SELF-AWARENESS	EMPATHY
PURPOSE	TEAM PLAY
INITIATIVE	RESILIENCE
PLANNING	SELF-CARE
COMMUNICATION	

Further Reading

Here is a list of sources that you can refer to should you wish to read further about the women leaders discussed in the book, their challenging lives and their many achievements. Despite their extensive body of work and unparalleled grit and bravery, these women have often been left out of popular discourse. This book is an attempt to fill this gap.

Books

Bonnie G. Smith, *The Oxford Encyclopedia of Women in World History* (Vol. 1), Oxford University Press, 2008.
Christopher Hibbert, *The Great Mutiny*, Penguin, 1980.
Ranjit S. Pandit, *Rajatarangini: The Saga Of The Kings Of Kasmir*, Sahitya Akademi, 2010.
William Dalrymple, *The Last Mughal: The Fall of a Dynasty, Delhi 1857*, Viking Penguin, 2006.

Online Sources

(Verified as of 20 February 2024)
https://theprint.in/features/rani-gaidinliu-daughter-of-the-hills-who-spent-14-years-in-jail-for-indias-independence/591570/
https://amritmahotsav.nic.in/unsung-heroes-detail.htm?56
https://sivaganga.nic.in/tourism/eminent-personalities/
https://www.livehistoryindia.com/story/people/velu-nachiyar
https://ignca.gov.in/abbakka-rani-the-unsung-warrior-queen/
https://www.thebetterindia.com/115196/rani-abbaka-chowta-ullal-tulu-nadu-karnataka/
https://www.allaboutsikhs.com/biographies/great-sikh-women/mai-bhago/
https://artsandculture.google.com/entity/mai-bhago/m0gn752?hl=en
https://www.livehistoryindia.com/story/people/mai-bhago-the-great-sikh-warrior
https://kaurlife.org/2022/01/04/mai-bhago/
https://indianculture.gov.in/stories/begum-hazrat-mahal-revolutionary-queen-awadh
https://www.livehistoryindia.com/story/people/begum-hazrat-mahal-a-revolutionary-queen
https://www.livehistoryindia.com/herstory/2017/07/17/rani-durgavati-the-warrior-queen-of-the-gonds
https://feminisminindia.com/2019/06/24/rani-durgavati-gond-queen/
https://modeindia.co.in/special_days/birthday-of-rani-durgavati/
https://archive.org/details/in.ernet.dli.2015.55649/page/n333/mode/2up?view=theater&q=sher+shah+suri

Ilina Singh

Ilina writes books for young readers who like to think for themselves as they explore and understand their world. Her first book – *The Gutsy Girls of Science* – was written in partnership with UNESCO and told the stories of Indian women scientists who were pioneers in their fields.

As Ilina started her college applications, she often encountered a common question across colleges – how had she displayed leadership and what did the word mean to her? Interestingly, her research pointed to the fact that there is no cookie-cutter definition of leadership. Leaders are not born, but made. Yet, young children are often not encouraged to imagine themselves as leaders. In particular, young girls are seldom expected to take up roles of authority.

Ilina was motivated when a family friend, Mr Rajat Banerji, pointed out to her that India has had a tradition of powerful female leaders. As she researched the lives of these queens and freedom fighters, she was struck by the leadership lessons that young children could use to kickstart their own leadership journeys. The result is this book and the nine-step leadership framework, which is the first comprehensive leadership module for children. Ilina stays in Gurgaon with her parents and her pet dog, Uzi. She enjoys painting, travelling and dancing.

I'd like to thank the wonderful team at HarperCollins who not only believed in the book, but made it so much better. Tina, Ankita and Isha - you are the dream team.

—Ilina Singh

Other Timeless Biographies by HarperCollins

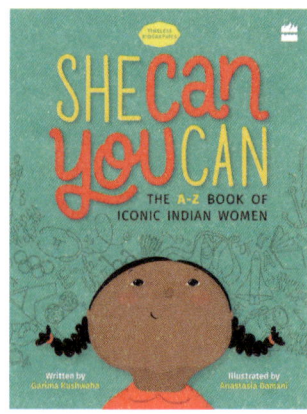
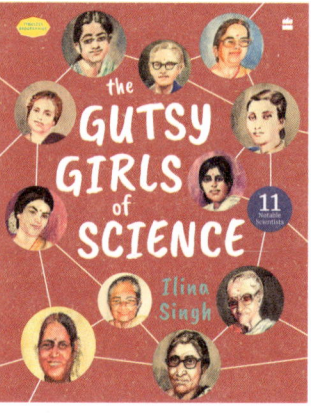
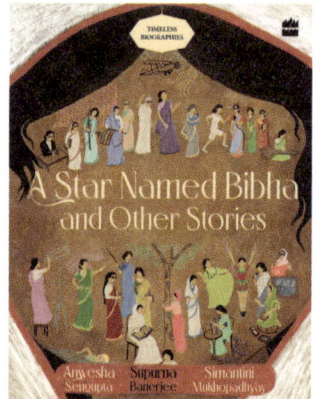